WILD HORSES
Running Free

LINDA L. RICHARDS

ORCA BOOK PUBLISHERS

Published in Canada and the United States
in 2023 by Orca Book Publishers.
orcabook.com

Library and Archives Canada Cataloguing in Publication
Title: Wild horses : running free / Linda L. Richards.
Names: Richards, Linda L. (Linda Lea), 1960- author.
Series: Orca wild ; 11.
Description: Series statement: Orca wild ; 11 |
Includes bibliographical references and index.
Identifiers: Canadiana (print) 20220496277 |
Canadiana (ebook) 20220496285 | ISBN 9781459825598 (hardcover) |
ISBN 9781459825604 (PDF) | ISBN 9781459825611 (EPUB)
Subjects: LCSH: Wild horses—Juvenile literature.
Classification: LCC SF360 .R53 2023 | DDC j599.665/5—dc23

Library of Congress Control Number: 2022950783

Summary: Part of the nonfiction Orca Wild series for middle-grade
readers and illustrated with color photographs throughout,
this book looks at the controversial past, present and future
of wild horses around the world, including the ongoing
threats to their existence.

Orca Book Publishers is committed to reducing the
consumption of nonrenewable resources in the production
of our books. We make every effort to use materials that
support a sustainable future.

Orca Book Publishers gratefully acknowledges the
support for its publishing programs provided by the following
agencies: the Government of Canada, the Canada Council
for the Arts and the Province of British Columbia through
the BC Arts Council and the Book Publishing Tax Credit.

The author and publisher have made every effort to
ensure that the information in this book was correct
at the time of publication. The author and publisher
do not assume any liability for any loss, damage, or
disruption caused by errors or omissions. Every effort has
been made to trace copyright holders and to obtain their
permission for the use of copyrighted material. The
publisher apologizes for any errors or omissions and would
be grateful if notified of any corrections that should be
incorporated in future reprints or editions of this book.

Front cover photo by
Lori Sortino/Essence Captured Photography
Design by Jenn Playford
Cover design by Dahlia Yuen
Edited by Kirstie Hudson

Printed and bound in South Korea.

26 25 24 23 • 1 2 3 4

Spirit is the Kiger mustang who was the muse for the iconic 2002
DreamWorks animated film *Spirit: Stallion of the Cimarron*. Today
Spirit lives at Return to Freedom, a wild horse sanctuary in California.
LORI SORTINO/ESSENCE CAPTURED PHOTOGRAPHY

With flowing tail and flying mane,
Wide nostrils never stretched by pain,
Mouths bloodless to the bit or rein,
And feet that iron never shod,
And flanks unscarred by spur or rod,
A thousand horse, the wild, the free,
Like waves that follow o'er the sea,
Came thickly thundering on.
—*Lord Byron*

CONTENTS

One

WHAT'S A WILD HORSE, ANYWAY?

Two

MEET THE WILD HORSE

Three

THE AMERICAN MUSTANG: HOW IT ALL BEGAN

WILD HORSES EVERYWHERE

THE MODERN MUSTANG

Various sources say that there are 22 wild horse herds galloping through the wilds of Utah, in the American West.
GEORGECLERK/GETTY IMAGES

Introduction

HORSES EVERYWHERE

When I was growing up, my bedroom was full of horses. Stuffed and soft. Smooth and plastic. Frozen in poses—jumping and running and forever on the edge of action. They had names, these well-loved pretend equines positioned on the shelves my father was forced to build to house my ever-growing stable.

Books were part of my obsession. *The Black Stallion* by Walter Farley, *Black Beauty* by Anna Sewell, *Misty of Chincoteague* by Marguerite Henry, and others. I was horse crazy. I lived and dreamed and breathed horses. And I was lucky. When I was 12, real-life living and breathing horses came into my life when my family bought 20 acres in a community known to be horsey. Aside from the information I'd taken in through books and the rides I'd gone on at every opportunity, I didn't really know anything about horses. But now that I lived on an acreage, I knew a horse would be in my future. I just hadn't figured out how it would happen. Then one day not long after we'd moved there, Bonnie showed up.

Here I am with the "mustang" mare, Bonnie, many years ago.
KARL HUBER

MY VERY OWN MUSTANG!

Bonnie was a bright sorrel with a white *blaze*, and she wouldn't let anyone near her. My dad figured she had been living on the armed forces base across the street or even somewhere on our property. She was beautiful. I consulted books and magazines and determined that, as unlikely as this would be in Langley, British Columbia, she must be a wild mustang.

To my eye she had all the characteristics! She had an abundant mane that erupted on either side of her beautiful neck. To me, the way she was put together—stocky body, sturdy legs—looked just like the mustangs in my books. I would race home after school to see if she was there. Sometimes she was. Then I'd move toward her—gently, gently, exactly as I'd read, trying to gain her trust and friendship.

It didn't take long before she let me get close enough to feel her smooth coat under my fingertips and catch a whiff of her horsey smell. My excitement grew as I realized I was taming a wild horse! I marveled at my amazing mustang-taming abilities. I was a natural. It wasn't long before I slipped a halter over her head. Not long after that, I bravely led her near a big rock and slid onto her back. She didn't buck me off. I had tamed my wild mustang.

Except my wild mustang turned out not to be. We discovered that Bonnie belonged to a farmer a few miles away. She'd escaped her pen months before. One day a horse trailer pulled up and loaded the "mustang" I'd called Bonnie and took her away. I was heartbroken, but my future would have other horses—lots of them. I would ride in competitions and, for a while, make horses my life and career. But I'd never forget my "mustang" Bonnie, who, though not an actual mustang, embodied the spirit, connection and idea of one.

WILD HORSES AROUND THE WORLD

Growing up, I identified most strongly with the American mustang found in the western United States, but that is not the only place wild horses can be found. They exist almost everywhere, though their stories are very different. Some of these horses have always been wild. Others are descended from domestic horses left behind on expeditions when they were no longer needed. And some, like ones in Scotland and other places in the United Kingdom and Europe, have been reintroduced to areas where there were no longer any wild horses and people wanted them back again.

TELLING A DIFFERENT STORY

This book didn't end up being what I'd thought it would be when I began. As I researched, a different picture from the one I had imagined emerged. I was surprised to find that some people in North America don't want wild horses. Not because they don't like horses (who doesn't like horses?!?) but because wild horses interfere with how they want to use the land—for things like oil extraction and mining. Also, people who use public land to graze their livestock believe that wild horses compete with their cattle or sheep for food and that their animals have more right to the land than the horses do.

I started out wanting to report only the beauty and inspiration of wild horses. It turns out there is so much more to their story than that. In the American West that story is complicated. But I hope you will come to see why their preservation in the wild is not only possible but can benefit all of us.

The wild horses of the Onaqui Mountain Herd Management Area in Utah are among the most popular and well-known of the American mustang bands, drawing visitors from all over the country.
KEVIN RUSS/GETTY IMAGES

In their natural habitat, wild horses are mostly cautious of people, but they can also be curious, seeming to wonder what nearby humans might be up to.
ROB PALMER PHOTOGRAPHY/SHUTTERSTOCK.COM

One

What's a Wild Horse, Anyway?

HORSES ARE SPECIAL

Everybody loves horses. The flowing mane and tail. Those big, lovely eyes and long, delicate legs. Horses make us think of strength and speed and the sense of flight we can enjoy when we ride.

We think horses are beautiful. Because of this, they seem to touch us on an emotional level. If they were ugly or funny-looking—like the northern elephant seal, the subject of my last book—the story of wild horses in the modern world would be totally different. But we look at them and see freedom and reminders of our history.

ENTER *EQUUS*

Everything that is shaped like a horse shares common ancestry. Even though some wild and domestic horses look very different from each other, they are all in the **genus** *Equus*, the only recognized **extant** genus in the family Equidae. *Equus* comprises seven living species and numerous extinct species known only through fossils. The genus includes horses, donkeys and zebras.

This restoration of *Sifrhippus sandrae* is in the Swedish Museum of Natural History (Naturhistoriska riksmuseet) in Stockholm.
EDUARD SOLÀ/WIKIMEDIA COMMONS/
CC BY-SA 3.0

The ancient and extinct horses in this vintage sketch are from different eras. The *Mesohippus, Neohipparion, Eohippus, Equus scotti* and *Hypohippus* horses would never have roamed together, but they are illustrated here for scale.
HEINRICH HARDER/WIKIMEDIA COMMONS/
PUBLIC DOMAIN

Wild horses are classified as *Equus ferus*, and there are three subspecies of *Equus ferus* on Earth today. The wild horse is *Equus ferus ferus*. The modern domestic horse is *Equus ferus caballus*, and the endangered Przewalski's horse, thought to be the only truly wild species left, is *Equus ferus przewalskii*. A number of other subspecies of *Equus* are now extinct—some fairly recently, some in prehistory.

HORSES IN PREHISTORY

Sifrhippus sandrae: All members of genus *Equus* can trace their family tree back to **Sifrhippus sandrae**, the oldest horse in the fossil record. *Sifrhippus* was an **ungulate** that lived early in the Eocene **epoch**, a time about 55 million years ago when the earth was warm and humid. There weren't many grasslands then, and forests were almost everywhere. *Sifrhippus* was a **browser**, meaning it ate leaves from trees, fruits of high-growing woody plants, soft shoots and shrubs. *Sifrhippus* looked a lot like modern horses but was much smaller and quite thin. It probably weighed between 8 and 12 pounds (4 to 6 kilograms). Just 12 inches (30 centimeters) tall at its largest, it had a close, shorthaired coat, like the modern horse, and a long head and jaw. Its front feet had four toes and the back feet had three. Its size variance, according to one theory, depended on the warmth of the climate. The warmer the environment got, the smaller the horses became, which scientists think may have been part of natural selection. Later in the early Eocene epoch, tiny horses would include *Eohippus* in North America and *Hyracotherium* in Europe.

Mesohippus: Next on the evolutionary road that leads to the modern horse was *Mesohippus*, which lived around 40 to 30 million years ago. Its name is from the Greek *mess*, which means "middle," and *hippos*, which means "horse." *Mesohippus* was tridactyl, which means it had three toes on each foot, while *Eohippus* had four on the front feet and three on the back. Fewer toes meant *Mesohippus* could do a better job of running away from **predators**. Things were definitely moving in the right direction!

Eohippus, or "dawn horse," is thought by some experts to be the earliest ancestor of the modern horse in North America. In Europe at the same time a very similar animal has been labeled as *Hyracotherium*.
DANIEL ESKRIDGE/SHUTTERSTOCK.COM

An Ass by Any Other Name

MOELYN PHOTOS/GETTY IMAGES

Let's just get the giggles out of the way right now. The word *ass*—no matter how it's used—has its root in *Equus africanus asinus*. The Swedish botanist Carl Linnaeus (1707–1778) came up with the name, maybe because he was good at naming things. He is probably more famous for the stuff he named than for any of the interesting things he did. Without him, I can't think what we'd be calling all this stuff. "That brown thing over there that whinnies." So before you make an ass of yourself (sorry), remember Carl Linnaeus and all the love and energy he put into naming... everything!

ALEXANDER ROSLIN/WIKIMEDIA COMMONS/ PUBLIC DOMAIN

Merychippus: This animal stood about 35 inches (89 centimeters) tall, which made it the largest of the horse ancestors to have lived up until that time. Also a three-toed horse, it was faster and sleeker than the horses who evolved during the middle and late Miocene epoch, 16–5.3 million years ago. Unlike the **equids** that had come before, *Merychippus* was a grazing animal very much like the modern horse—no more reaching up to get leaves from trees!

Pliohippus: *Pliohippus* appeared around 12 million years ago, in the middle Miocene epoch. It looked a lot like modern *Equus*, and until recently taxonomists thought *Pliohippus* was the ancestor of the modern horse. Now researchers realize that they are different in some important ways, like having curved teeth instead of straight.

Dinohippus: Present-day researchers now believe that *Dinohippus* (which means "terrible horse"!) might have been the true missing link between ancient and modern horses. *Dinohippus*, which was about 440 pounds (200 kilograms), appeared late in the Miocene epoch and is thought to be the most recent direct ancestor of *Equus*, the genus that includes the modern horse, zebras and **asses**. *Dinohippus* first appeared about 13.5 million years ago in North America. It was a grazing animal and was the first of the horse ancestors to show signs of the **stay apparatus** that is what enables horses to sleep while standing and stand for long periods of time without using much energy. Examples of *Dinohippus* have been found with multiple toes and also with a single toe ending in a hoof, like the modern horses we are used to seeing.

The Family Equidae

AIRSPA/GETTY IMAGES

DONKEYS

Equus asinu (African wild ass, donkey or burro)

Equus hemionus (kulan and onager)

FRANCES DE JONG/GETTY IMAGES

HORSES

Equus ferus (horse)

Equus ferus caballus (modern domestic horse)

Equus ferus ferus (wild horse)

EHRMAN PHOTOGRAPHIC/SHUTTERSTOCK.COM

ZEBRAS

Equus burchelli (Burchell's zebra)

Equus grevyi (Grevy's zebra)

Equus zebra (Mountain zebra)

LOUISLOTTERPHOTOGRAPHY/SHUTTERSTOCK.COM

QUAGGA

Equus quagga (the recently extinct quagga)

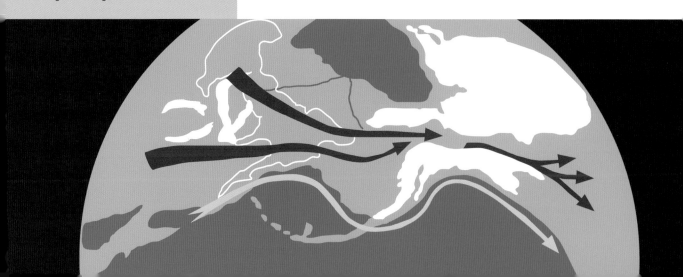

A chromosome is the package that contains an organism's genetic material. Every organism gets half of its genetic information from each parent.
DARRYL LEJA, NIH, NHGRI

This map shows how a part of Earth looked during the last ice age, around 18,000 years ago. Sea levels were much lower, allowing humans, horses and other creatures to migrate east across modern-day Asia and into North America using the Bering land bridge.

HISTORY ON ITS HAUNCHES

For a really long time, researchers used the horse as the ideal snapshot of how species evolve. More recently, however, new finds of ancient bones and **DNA** evidence have shown that maybe everything is not as clear as it once was. It turns out there have been more branches of the horse family and more genetic divisions along the way than experts previously believed. Also, some of the species further along the evolutionary path coexisted with **ancestor species**, which would have made things even more confusing for the researchers looking for evidence of the true prehistoric history of the horse.

Much of the horse's evolution took place in North America. At least a couple of times in prehistory, horses migrated across the Bering land bridge to Asia and then to Europe. For as long as people have studied the evolutionary history of horses, it was thought that the horse had become extinct in North America after these migrations, only to be reintroduced fairly recently in history—about 400 years ago. A lot of history books still say that. But there is growing evidence that horses have been here all along. And more evidence still that even if they weren't here the whole time, they originally evolved in North America.

Bureau of Land Management

To reduce the size of herds, horses are sometimes chased by helicopter into holding pens.
BLM NEVADA/FLICKR.COM/CC BY 2.0

You can't really talk much about wild horses in the American West without hearing about the **Bureau of Land Management (BLM)**. A division of the US Department of the Interior, the BLM is responsible for administering public lands. The BLM manages one in every 10 acres (4.05 hectares) of land in the United States and approximately 30 percent of the country's minerals. The lands and minerals are found in every state and encompass forests, mountains, rangelands, arctic tundra and deserts.

According to the American Wild Horse Campaign, the BLM manages 245 million acres (99 million hectares) of public land in the United States. Livestock grazing is authorized on 155 million (63 million hectares) of those acres, while wild horses and burros are restricted to 26.9 million acres (11 million hectares) of the BLM land.

So that's a lot of millions of acres, but it means the amount of land wild horses have access to is roughly 10 percent of the amount allotted to livestock. To make matters worse, a lot of those acres that the horses are on are also shared with livestock.

The BLM believes the land can support only 26,785 wild horses, even though right now there are 80,000 on the range. Many organizations supporting the American wild horse consider the BLM figure too low, saying that their research indicates more horses could be supported on the range.

And while the BLM says the horses are "restricted" to those certain areas, what that actually means is different in different places. For example, the wild horses considered part of the Salt River management area in Arizona are confined by fences and cattle guards to keep them from wandering onto roads. In Montana, some bands of wild horses just don't read the signs and, without any fences, have been known to clop right through the middle of towns. However the "restrictions" are accomplished, it's worth remembering that the areas we are talking about are really, really big and the number of horses can be assumed, in many cases, to be an estimate.

What's a Hoof?

PEOPLEIMAGES/GETTY IMAGES

A hoof is the tip of the toe of an ungulate animal. On a horse, the hoof is that hard, keratinized protein shoe on the end of each toe. Our hair and nails are made of keratin. Horses' hooves are made out of the same stuff. In the hoof, though, keratin is laid in horizontal bands that make up the superstrong toe that will support the whole horse. Horses are the only animal with a single toe, but evidence remains of the toes that evolution left behind.

A biologist at the University of Massachusetts, Dartmouth, discovered what she felt was proof that earlier in their evolution, horses had five toes. Kathryn Kavanagh was working with preserved horse embryos. She noted that very early in its pre-birth development, a *foal* has clusters of developing cells representing toes.

"We think it wasn't recognized before because the appearance was so brief," Kavanagh told the *New York Times*. "[The stage at which the clusters are visible] only lasts a couple of days, and we got really lucky."

The embryo has all the horse instructions to begin with. As it grows, it sheds the instructions not useful to the modern horse. The same is true for humans. Early in development, human embryos have gills and a tail, showing the evolutionary path we have taken too.

NEW CHAPTERS IN HISTORY

In 2017, while having landscape work done in their yard, a Utah couple discovered bones on their property. They figured the bones were from a cow. Their neighbor, a professor of geology at nearby Brigham Young University, looked at the bones and told them they were from a horse, probably from the Pleistocene era. The bones were sent to a lab to be examined and DNA tested. They were about 16,000 years old!

Once researchers had reconstructed the bones, they discovered that the animals had been seen before—fossils of these stilt-legged horses had been excavated from other sites, including the Natural Trap Cave in Wyoming, Gypsum Cave in Nevada and the Klondike goldfields in Yukon. They're called *stilt-legged* because their legs were longer and thinner than the legs of other horses of the time.

Even though other examples of the stilt-legged horses that had been found in Utah were uncovered—and all were between 13,000 and 16,000 years old—DNA testing proved they were unrelated to any living horses. They called the newly discovered species *Haringtonhippus francisci*.

Feet are the foundation. They provide support. Look how these different animals are supported by what's underneath. OLGA KURBATOVA/GETTY IMAGES

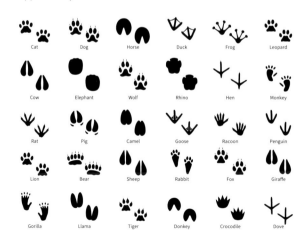

The Eyes Have It: How Horses See

The eyes of a horse are larger than those of any other land mammal. And those big eyes are designed to help them see day and night. The horse's *retina* is large too. In addition to bringing in extra light, this superlarge retina acts as a magnifying glass. When you see something, a horse will see the same thing, except it will appear to be bigger and closer than it looks to you.

In addition to having the largest eyes, horses also have the widest field of view. Because their eyes are on the sides of their head, horses mostly have monocular vision. You and I have strictly binocular vision—our eyes are positioned on the front of our face. We can see really well straight ahead, but we have to turn our head to see what is beside us. Plus, our eyes work together. Horses can operate each eye separately. Because of that, they get a bonus of some binocular vision too. In fact, with this full monocular vision and partial binocular vision, horses can almost see all around them.

We were built to hunt, so we need all of our focus ahead—on our target. Horses, on the other hand, are built to observe the slightest change in their surroundings, then run away when some unusual movement occurs. Although the position of their eyes gives them almost 360-degree vision, the placement also means there is a blind spot directly in front of the horse and another near its bum. But these blind spots are small. There's not much that will escape their attention.

Horses can only see two of the visible wavelengths in the light spectrum, allowing them to see all shades of blue and green, but not red.

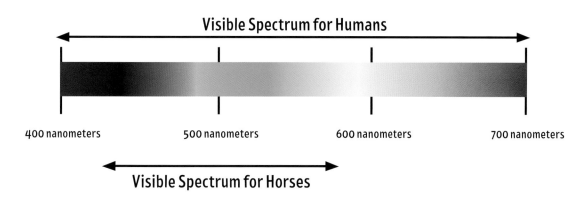

In the wild, horse families are tightly structured.
TWILDLIFE/GETTY IMAGES

Two

Meet the Wild Horse

SOCIAL ANIMALS

Horses are deeply social creatures. They are *herd* animals and are happiest when they are around other horses. The herd—the family—is everything. In the wild the individual is second. The herd must survive. It has to move and function like a single creature. One horse can't just wander off alone. If it does, the senior *stallion* or the boss *mare* will get it in line. A boss horse uses vocalizations, the weight of its body or gentle nips and kicks to bring the offender back into the bunch.

Horses are wonderful companions for humans because of their herd instinct. That's why humans have been able to forge such great partnerships with them. In the wild their lives depend on conforming to the rules of their social order. They are used to following the instructions of animals with more status in their community. This prepares them to listen to human partners when they are no longer in the wild.

In captivity, domestic horses respond to the humans who care for them in much the same way they would have responded to the *alpha* members of their herd. They look to their human partners to keep them safe and provide what is needed for their survival.

IT'S ALL IN THE FAMILY

In the wild, horses have a social structure. The safety and well-being of the herd depends on everyone doing their part. And this structure is as it has always been for members of genus *Equus*. Here's how the horse family is structured in the wild.

The Herd Stallion

A **dominant**, or senior, stallion leads each **band** of horses. He is the boss of everyone in the herd. It is his responsibility to look out for his herd—to keep them safe from predators and other dangers. He also sires all the foals, or baby horses, that will be born to the herd.

In the wild a dominant male horse has to fight for the right to lead and breed with a **harem** of mares. These fights are seldom deadly and often involve body language and vocalizations as much as physical conflict, though there is often some of that too. To lead a herd, the stallion has to inspire confidence in the animals he is leading. Only the strongest and bravest stallions are able to maintain the position.

Fights between stallions are seldom lethal. They scream at each other and make lunges as though to bite and kick. A lot of it is for show. It lets both horses know who would win if things ever got serious.
TWILDLIFE/GETTY IMAGES

The Beta Stallion

Horse herds don't always have a **beta** stallion. When they do, he will be a younger stallion who acts something like an assistant to the herd stallion. He'll help keep males from outside the herd away. He won't mate with the mature mares in the band, but he may mate with daughters of the senior stallion or with mares from other bands who might drift into the group.

The Boss Mare

The stallion is not alone at the head of the herd. He shares responsibility with the lead or boss mare. She is usually one of the oldest mares and is the one the rest of the herd trusts and respects the most. She determines the direction the herd takes when it travels. When the horses reach water, she'll drink first. It's her job to find the best food sources and help the stallions keep an eye out for danger.

The lead mare helps make sure the herd stays safe and finds the resources needed, like food and water.
SOMOGYVARI/GETTY IMAGES

A traditional herd of wild horses—one that has been allowed to develop without human intervention—will splinter into subgroups as the herd matures and grows.
LINDA L. RICHARDS

The Bachelor Band

As the *colts* in the herd mature, they become threats to the boss stallion. Before they are strong enough to challenge their father, he will run them off. These young males don't have mares to hang out with. But because horses are social animals and don't like to be alone, the young males—and also older males who are not strong or dominant enough to command a herd of their own—hang out together. This group of single males is a satellite to the main herd and is known as a bachelor band. The bachelor band is separate from the main herd but never very far away. It functions like a well-defined part of the main herd—the horses have a clear understanding of where they fit in the family structure.

LORI SORTINO/ESSENCE CAPTURED PHOTOGRAPHY

The Mares

The main part of a wild horse band will consist of 2 to 25 mares, plus offspring that are one to one and a half years old.

When the herd is traveling, you'll quite often see mares with foals at their sides. Foals from the year before—the yearlings—also travel with the herd, though not at their mother's side. Those older colts and *fillies* (young females) will form their own subgroup within the herd. (Teenagers hanging out together!) When the herd gets larger, because adult mares are added or fillies grow to adulthood, the herd splinters into smaller groups.

All horses, wild or not, enjoy the company of others of their kind. Horses are deeply social animals.
LINDA L. RICHARDS

A Name for the Genders

Stallion: Unneutered male of breeding age

Gelding: Male who has been *neutered* and is not able to sire foals

Mare: Adult female

Colt: Juvenile male

Filly: Juvenile female

Foal: A horse under one year of age, of either gender

FORM TO FUNCTION

When trying to understand horses, it's helpful to remember that they evolved as a prey animal. That means they were meant to be hunted, not be the hunter. Because of this, their first instinct when faced with danger is to run away.

The natural predators of horses are large animals like wolves, cougars and bears. The ability to outrun these animals has been important throughout the horse's evolution, and it's why, as horses evolved, they became able to run faster and faster.

As a prey species, their survival in the wild depends on their ability to know when predators are stalking them. Horses are extremely sensitive to changes in the environment around them and have the ability to respond to those changes quickly. Everything about the way horses have evolved contributes to their ability to be hyperaware.

The eyes of a horse are positioned in a way that gives the animal almost 360-degree vision. MARTIN GALLAGHER/GETTY IMAGES

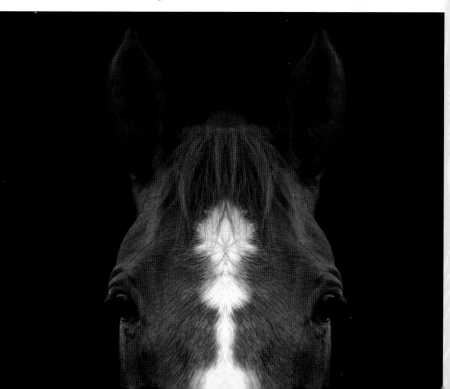

When Is a Horse a Pony? When Is a Pony a Horse?

ASYAPOZNIAK/GETTY IMAGES

The word *pony* might make you picture some tiny pet of a horse, maybe the size of a big dog. Some people think a pony is simply a foal or young horse. It is not. *Pony* is a size designation only, and a pony can be of any age. In horse lingo, though, *pony* means a few specific and different things.

Officially, in show-horse and breeding circles in North America, a pony is any horse that is under 14.2 **hands** (56.8 inches or 144 centimeters). Ponies are also considered a **phenotype**, meaning that environmental factors—like little or inferior food, small quarters or hard conditions—interacted with their genetic makeup, forcing them to be smaller than other horses.

To confuse things further, some recognized horse breeds are often not horse-sized by these definitions. The Morgan, the Arabian and the American quarter horse, for example, can often be classified as ponies by their size alone. Many wild horses are pony-sized too, possibly because they have to spend so much of their energy scrabbling for resources.

Another confusing piece: Pony Club—an international youth organization promoting equestrian values internationally—considers horses of all sizes to be ponies if they are ridden by juniors.

As we read in chapter 1, their eyes are designed and positioned to see as much of their environment at one time as possible.

A horse's hearing is similar in range and tone to that of humans, but much more sharp. A horse can hear very low and very high frequencies. Using 10 different muscles, a horse can rotate its ears 180 degrees. This unique anatomical feature allows horses to focus their ears on the direction the sound is coming from, isolate it and run the other way if necessary.

Another part of being a prey species is that foals are born precocial. That means they are born with an advanced level of maturity, capable of independent activity. A newly born foal will be up and running with the herd within hours. Compare this with humans, who are born altricial. Unlike other primates (and horses!), we are born helpless and need caregivers to do everything for us for years.

Because horses hear so well, the smallest sound can alert them to a change in their environment. LINDA L. RICHARDS

HORSES DON'T LIVE IN THE FOREST

Though the earliest ancestor of the horse, *Eohippus,* or *Hyracotherium*, was forest-dwelling, modern horses don't live in forests. Why? Because in the forest, predators like big cats can lurk in the trees above them, and other animals can sneak up on them. And although horses might fight against each other in certain situations, they don't use their teeth or hooves to defend themselves against predators unless they're cornered. They're built for speed, and in emergency situations they use it and run away. They have evolved from being a little woodland dweller at a time when the world was mostly covered with forest to running in huge herds on the open plains.

Those who have spent time riding domestic horses may have seen this instinctive aversion to forest trails from their **equine** partners. Horses have to learn to be comfortable under the cover of dense trees. They have to be made to understand that nothing will pounce on them from above. Horses ridden in forest conditions are taught this as part of their training.

A HOME FOR HORSES

On the open range, a horse herd can travel 30 to 40 miles (45 to 65 kilometers) a day. In most places in the world today, however, wild horses are restricted by some sort of real or imposed boundary. They are fenced into a large area, or their movement is restricted by roads and vehicles and towns.

Wild horses cherish their freedom. They mostly just want to be left alone, and they avoid human contact. In storms on the open plains, wild horse herds will take

Wild horses in this group in the Apache-Sitgreaves National Forests in Arizona peek out at the author from behind a tree. Though horses generally prefer open ground, sparsely treed forests are part of the habitat of these horses.
LINDA L. RICHARDS

shelter with one another, forming a circle with their butts to the storm and their heads together to get the protection from the elements that they need.

WHAT DO WILD HORSES EAT?

Horses eat seeds and grasses. When their preferred foods are difficult to find, they'll eat bark and wood. There have been stories of horses eating small prey animals and scavenging off dead animal flesh. But if that's true, it's unusual. There are also stories about riders whose mounts have stolen the occasional hamburger or chicken sandwich. But it's not part of their normal diet, as horses are *not* built to eat meat.

The type of *herbaceous* things they eat depends on where the horses live. Desert mustangs will work hard at finding enough dry grasses to eat year round. They'll also strip the bark off certain trees and nibble at leaves and *forbs*. A University of Wyoming rangeland study showed that the wild horses in that region ate sagebrush, greasewood, saltbush, juniper, perennial bunchgrass, wheatgrass, *sedges* and needlegrass. The wild horses in the United Kingdom eat reeds, weeds and whatever grasses they can find. And Canada's Sable Island horses eat the nutrient-rich grasses fertilized by the growing seal population on the island.

Wild horses eat what is available to them. And all of them, no matter where they are, spend almost all of their time close to fresh water, partly because they need it to survive and partly because, no matter where they are, the kinds of weeds and grasses horses thrive on grow best near water.

Wild horses eat almost constantly—14 to 18 hours a day.
ANNIE SPRATT/UNSPLASH.COM

Horses on the Menu

A recent study showed that, in certain circumstances, size doesn't matter. If they're hungry enough, cougars will happily make a meal out of horses. NATURESFAN1226/WIKIMEDIA COMMONS/CC BY 3.0

For a long time it was thought that cougars didn't prey on mustangs very often. How could they? The average mustang weighs about 850 pounds (385 kilograms). The average male cougar weighs about 150 pounds (68 kilograms), and females may weigh a third less. Cougars aren't pack hunters. So how could such a small animal kill one so much larger? And why would they want to when their favorite food, mule deer—which each weigh between 130 and 280 pounds (59 and 127 kilograms)— are in such good supply and an easier target?

The Great Basin is a geographic region that includes nearly all of Nevada, a big portion of Utah and parts of California, Idaho, Oregon, Wyoming, and Baja California in Mexico. The region has an arid climate and a varied topography.

Scientists had heard stories of cougars eating horses in the Great Basin. In 2009 two researchers led a three-year study to find out if horses were actively being hunted or if some of the big cats were just scavenging on dead animals they came across. A team led by Jon Beckmann, a wildlife supervisor at the Kansas Department of Wildlife and Parks, and Alyson Andreasen, then a PhD student at the University of Nevada, Reno, put GPS collars on 21 cougars. Thirteen of the cougars were in the Great Basin. A control group of eight was in the Sierra Nevada mountain range. What they discovered startled everyone. While it turned out that mule deer made up 91 percent of the prey killed by the cats in the Sierra Nevada, the deer made up only 29 percent of kills in the Great Basin. The diet of cougars in the Great Basin was composed predominantly of horses. Interestingly, Great Basin female cougars killed more horses, of all ages, whereas male cougars tended to focus on weaker members of the horse bands. The researchers figured the females might be more motivated to take down big prey because they had kittens to feed.

From an early age, wild horses devote a lot of their time to eating.
RAYMOND SALMON/GETTY IMAGES

GROCERY SHOPPING

While I was sharing my life and small acreage with half a dozen horses, a friend came from the city to visit. She brought along someone who had never been around horses. When they arrived, the horses came to the fence to greet the visitors.

The non-horsey friend of a friend was overwhelmed by the attention of half a dozen 1,000-pound (454-kilogram) lookie-loos. "Oh my gosh," John said as we joined the horses at the fence. "It must cost you a fortune to feed these guys! How do you manage?"

"Well, yeah," I said, considering. "Alfalfa hay has gotten pretty expensive." That was the high-protein hay I'd been feeding the horses. "But it's not that bad."

The guest looked at me blankly for a minute, then said, "No, no. I mean, they're so big! Don't they eat a lot of meat?"

I had a moment of thinking about what a predator horse would look like. So scary!

Some animals are pure carnivores—like lions and elephant seals and house cats. Many animals are omnivores—like bears and dogs and humans. But horses are pure herbivores—like iguanas and goats and deer. Their digestive tract is set up to handle grasses and wild oats and hay. Horses are the classic "grazer" in that they are designed to eat small amounts of food frequently or even constantly. When horses aren't running or sleeping, they have their heads down foraging.

A wild horse will graze between 14 and 18 hours a day. An adult horse of medium size will eat between 5 and 6 pounds (about 2.5 kilograms) of herbaceous foods each day. That's a lot of ripping at sparse weeds and chewing. The horse needs small amounts of food over long periods just to keep everything working properly.

A Name for the Colors

Appaloosa: Dark spots on a white base

Bay: Any shade of brown but with black mane and tail

Black: A black with no red or brown in it; can appear blue

Buckskin: Bright gold with black mane, tail and *points*

Chestnut: A deep, rich brown, with mane and tail close to the same color as the body

Dun: Yellow or tan with a dark *dorsal stripe*, black mane, tail, ears and muzzle, and sometimes zebra-like stripes on the legs

Gray: Gray or white; gray horses are born black and lighten with age

Grulla: Like dun but with a bluish cast to the coat

Palamino: Gold with white mane and tail

Pinto: Splashes or splotches of white on a dark base

Roan: Any color but with flecks of white throughout the coat

A wild mare and her foal.
BRYANT AARDEMA—BRYANTS WILDLIFE
IMAGES/GETTY IMAGES

Three

The American Mustang:
How It All Began

MULTIPLE TRUTHS

The history of the American mustang is filled with myth and mystery. We can make good guesses about their story, but it's impossible to know the whole truth. What we do know is that in prehistory, horses evolved in North America before they were anywhere else. Then something happened, and they all disappeared. Or maybe they mostly disappeared—with just a few small pockets of them surviving. No one can be totally sure of that part.

The word *mustang* comes from the Spanish word *mustengo*. In ancient Spanish the word meant "ownerless beast" or "stray horse." In the earliest North American histories told by non-Indigenous people, it was claimed that there had never been horses on the continent at all prior to the arrival of Christopher Columbus and the other Europeans who followed him. Columbus arrived in North America in 1492 with three ships. Columbus's goal was to colonize the land, converting the existing inhabitants to Christianity and claiming the land for Spain. On those ships was land transportation—horses.

Some of the horses Columbus brought on his four expeditions escaped, and some were simply left behind to fend for themselves when the ships headed back to Spain. Those horses became *feral*. They're thought to be the ancestors of mustangs today.

On later voyages, the Spanish colonizers brought more horses to start breeding farms in order to have lots of land transport and also so they didn't need to keep bringing horses every time they came. Those horses were later joined by ones brought to North America by other Europeans. Again, people would leave some horses behind, saving space on their ships for goods from their travels. Some of the horses got loose and reverted to wild ways.

This painting by unknown artists depicts the conquest of the city of Tenochtitlán by the conquistadors. Tenochtitlán is now the site of Mexico City. The painting shows the battle between the Spanish and the Indigenous people.
SMITH ARCHIVE/ALAMY STOCK PHOTO

But there are scholars who say this isn't true. They say that there have always been horses in North America, and these Spanish ones just added to the gene pool that was already here. They say that horses were always part of the cultures of many of the Indigenous Peoples of the land that Europeans would come to call Canada, the United States and Mexico.

READING THE BONES

A paleontologist named Edward Drinker Cope found the remains of what he believed to be an ancient horse in Texas in 1892. Then, in 1930, Smithsonian paleontologist James W. Gidley discovered ancient horse remains at Hagerman, Idaho.

At first scholars did not believe them. How could there be ancient horse bones when there had never been horses? Eventually, though, the history books had to be rewritten. And so it came to be understood that horses had maybe even originated in North America but had died out or been killed by means no one has ever agreed upon. Some scholars think a big climate event happened. Others believe the horses were eaten by early humans. Still others believe it might have been a combination of these things, maybe aided by some genetic factor. But no one has ever agreed on why for sure. They agreed on only one thing: some big *extinction event*; then no horses in North America after that.

Many sources feel that bone evidence supporting horses having been in North America is always mounting, and now DNA evidence is being added.

The Hagerman horse is one of the oldest horses of the genus *Equus* and was discovered in 1928 in Hagerman, ID. It is recognized as the official state fossil of Idaho.
DADEROT/WIKIMEDIA COMMONS/ PUBLIC DOMAIN

Wild horses of the Brittany Triangle and the Nemiah Valley in the Chilcotin region of central British Columbia.
PATRICE HALLEY

ENTER NEMIAH

One of the examples of DNA tests changing the way we think about horse history in North America comes to us from the Chilcotin region of British Columbia. Recent DNA tests of wild horses in the mountainous 63,000-acre (155,000-hectare) area known as the Brittany Triangle show no relation to Spanish horses. Previously the wild horses in that area were thought to be descended from American mustangs who had made their way north. But it turns out the horses in the Brittany Triangle are not descended from the mustangs, and their special DNA suggests, in part, the possibility of a different ancestry.

Even before DNA isolated these horses as special, the Indigenous Peoples of the region had already determined they deserved special protection. In 2002 the Xeni Gwet'in First Nations Government established the Elegesi Qayus Wild Horse Preserve. It was the first of its kind in western Canada. Though the province of British Columbia still does not consider these horses as deserving special designation, since the preserve was declared the horses are monitored by wild horse rangers. The rangers are charged with providing surveillance and protection of the horses and other wild animals of the preserve.

HORSE SIGHTINGS FROM THE PAST

Wherever they came from, and whenever they first got here, domestic horses have been in North America for a long time. Early reports came from the Buddhist missionary Hui Shen. In the 5th century he traveled by boat from China to a land he called Fusang. Scholars in the 18th century argued—based on Hui Shen's reports of the journey—that Fusang was the west coast of North America extending from north of California to maybe as far north as British Columbia.

In her book *Chasing Their Dreams*, author Lily Chow writes that the Indigenous people Hui Shen found in Fusang "raised deer for meat and milk, just as the Chinese raised cattle at home, and produced cheese with deer milk. They traveled on horseback and transported their goods with carts or sledges pulled by horses, buffalo, or deer." Scholars scoffed, though. How could this be right? Everyone thought there were no horses in North America at that time.

Except Hui Shen's reports weren't the only ones.

In his book *Straight from the Horse's Heart*, R.T. Fitch reported that everywhere that explorers traveled along the eastern seaboard of North America during the 16th, 17th and 18th centuries, they reported seeing Welsh settlers and Indigenous Peoples riding horses. Fitch also writes

The Fusang tree as depicted in the mid-2nd century. Some scholars think the area described in Hui Shen's voyage was coastal British Columbia.
WIKIMEDIA COMMONS/PUBLIC DOMAIN

that in 1497, when Italian explorer John Cabot landed along the eastern coast of what would become Canada, he reported seeing horses and cattle, and that the horses and cattle would often be hidden from European eyes.

A DIFFERENT PICTURE

In 1535, when Jacques Cartier explored the region now called Quebec, his Haudenosaunee hosts told him there was a community of Indigenous people in the "Far West" who rode horses.

Fitch isn't alone in saying that at least some of the Indigenous people were careful to keep horses out of sight for fear they might be harmed, taken from them or killed. Dr. Yvette Running Horse Collin has studied the history of horses in North America and challenges all the known "truths" about wild horses.

However and whenever horses got to North America, they had become an important part of many Indigenous cultures by the second half of the 19th century.
CAMPWILLOWLAKE/GETTY IMAGES

Dr. Collin, who is an enrolled member of the Oglala Lakota Nation, says history as recorded is incorrect and that many Indigenous communities say they've had horses, along with well-established horse cultures, long before the arrival of the Spanish.

Other scholars don't agree. "Horses...originated in North America but went extinct," says E. Gus Cothran, a clinical professor at Texas A&M University School of Veterinary Medicine and Biomedical Sciences. "We aren't sure why. They returned with Columbus and the Spanish about 500 years ago. There is no solid fossil or archeological data to the contrary and all genetic data is consistent with this model."

And yet there are those stories, sightings, artifacts and detailed Indigenous knowledge that paint a different picture.

The Tolar Petroglyph Site is an archeological site in Sweetwater County, WY. The horse and rider here are thought to be Comanche. Wherever petroglyphs are located, it's difficult to determine their age.
S.L. KRAUSE/WIKIMEDIA COMMONS/ CC BY-SA 3.0

WHY IT MATTERS

There are many reasons it might have been important to defend the European version of the history of the horse in North America. In her work, Collin suggests that the Spanish explorers wanted to report back to their superiors that the Indigenous Peoples they encountered were not only horseless but also not skilled enough to have learned how to manage and control horses. It justified the actions of the Spanish colonizers—they thought they could take land and claim it for themselves, regardless of the original occupants. Also, if there were no horses in North America, the explorers could petition Queen Isabella I of Spain to supply a larger number of horses, including breeding animals, to be transported to what they were then calling the New World.

Ute petroglyphs near Wolfe Ranch and
Delicate Arch, in Arches National Park, UT.
JESSE THORNTON/ALAMY STOCK PHOTO

The experts do agree, though, that in the wild, horses evolved or adapted differently than their domestic cousins. Their hooves are stronger. There tends to be less variation in their physical characteristics. Domestic horses have a much larger range in size, from tiny ponies to huge draft animals. Wild horses are generally stocky, their ankles are more upright, their necks are shorter—all adaptations that make them suited for scrabbling up rocky hillsides and surviving rough desert trails. Wild horses have larger brains than their domestic cousins too. Maybe there is more thinking to do just to stay alive.

While there are exceptions, wild horses tend to bay, chestnut, dun and buckskin coloration, reverting over generations to the neutral colors of their ancestors. They blend in best with the desert and dry mountain areas that are their most natural habitat.

WILD OR FERAL: WHY IT MAKES A DIFFERENCE

In the United States and Canada, when it comes to wild horses, governments make a point of classifying horses as feral rather than wild. A feral animal is one that is descended from domestic animals but lives in the wild. Think Mowgli, the "man cub" from *The Jungle Book* who was raised by wolves. Mowgli was called a feral child because he was born of domesticated animals but was raised in the wild—he knew only wild ways.

But if horses have always been in North America—and that's a big *if*—they deserve to be protected as a native species. But because governments have classified wild horses as feral and, in some cases, even ***invasive***, they can be moved from what is otherwise their natural habitat.

The Jungle Book, written by Rudyard Kipling in the late 1800s, has been made into movies, plays and cartoons in many languages. It centers on Mowgli, a boy who is found in the jungle as a baby and raised by wolves.
WIKIMEDIA COMMONS/PUBLIC DOMAIN

Kids Saved the Wild Horses

ISPMB, KAREN A. SUSSMAN

There would be no debate over wild versus feral without the work of one woman, Velma Bronn Johnston. She essentially saved the wild horse in North America.

There was a time, in the 1960s, when when the future of the mustang was in serious danger. At that point the wild horse population in North America had dropped from its high point of two million about 100 years earlier to just 10,000 individuals. And things were getting worse.

Faced with an impossible situation, Velma Bronn Johnston—later known as "Wild Horse Annie"—stood up and did something.

Johnston had been raised on a ranch and worked as an executive secretary in Nevada. On her way to the office one morning, she saw blood dripping from the truck in front of her. Following it, she discovered that the truck was hauling a load of captured mustangs to the slaughterhouse. A yearling inside had fallen and was being trampled to death. She was horrified, but what shocked her even more was that this was legal in the United States at that time. She vowed to expose the cruel way the wild horses of North America were being hunted and captured, or sometimes poisoned or shot, and then *slaughtered* for dog food.

Johnston used all her organizational skills and contacts to tell the media how wild horses were being treated. She went to schools and wherever people gathered to talk about wild horses. Because of what she did, people wrote letters to important people in government—thousands came from grade-school children across the United States. Then the US Congress passed the Wild Free-Roaming Horses and Burros Act of 1971. The law protected the horses and guaranteed a life of freedom, free from cruelty. The law also provided for the necessary management, protection and control of wild horses and burros on public lands.

Wild Horse Annie's actions changed the future for wild horses in North America, yet it started so simply—and the children who wrote letters played a huge part.

Golden light shines on some of the mustangs
protected by the Return to Freedom sanctuary.
LORI SORTINO/ESSENCE CAPTURED PHOTOGRAPHY

Current numbers vary, but at time of writing there are between 60,000 and 80,000 horses that are considered mustangs on the nearly 27 million acres managed by the Bureau of Land Management (BLM) in the western United States. Whatever their history, these mustangs are hardy, surefooted and beautiful.

There are people who think we need to do everything we can to protect the mustangs and keep them wild. There are also people who say something has to be done about them—that they are bad for the environment, that they eat too much of the grass that deer or cattle or various other species need to eat, that there are too many of them.

A healthy horse herd will increase in size in the wild by 20 to 25 percent every year. Where there are 10,000 horses one year, there will be more than 12,000 the next. Which means around 15,000 the following year. Then 20,000 after that, and so on.

Some people argue that as the herd gets bigger, predators and nature will keep the population in check. Other people say the population of mustangs is growing too fast and their numbers should be controlled through such methods as birth control. For the moment, though, the American mustang continues. Indomitable as always.

Like animals of many species (including humans!), equine mothers and babies share a special bond.
OLGAIT/GETTY IMAGES

WHAT IS TRUE?

So are horses wild or feral? Were they introduced by Columbus? Or have they always been in North America? The Animal Welfare Institute, one of the oldest animal welfare organizations in the United States, maintains that it doesn't matter whether the horse has always been in North America. It has studies and evidence indicating that there is no significant difference between the ancient horses that lived in North America and the wild horses here now. That is, their habits, grazing patterns and interactions with the environment are the same as those of the prehistoric horses.

PART OF THE ENVIRONMENT

Some of the critics of America's wild horses and those who would like to see their numbers reduced say the herds are damaging the ranges where they are free. One of the reasons they give is that horses in North America are not natural and so don't belong wild on the range.

Wild horse advocates say that not only are horses not a threat to other wild species, but because they evolved in North America, as part of a system that works, their migration habits and the way they eat and move actually support other wild species. The theory is that other species benefit from the horses' style of grazing in a *symbiotic* way.

A SCIENTIFIC CONCLUSION

Researchers at the Paleogenomics Lab at the University of California Santa Cruz have determined that regardless of whether horses were in North America all along, DNA ties today's wild horses to the ancient horses that roamed the continent. Researchers concluded that American mustangs share much of their DNA and evolutionary history with their ancestors who lived on the same continent thousands of years earlier.

A beautiful roan stallion assesses his surroundings in Utah's Onaqui Mountain Herd Management Area.
TWILDLIFE/GETTY IMAGES

Picasso of Sand Wash Basin

Picasso, of Sand Wash Basin, was one of the most famous wild horses that ever lived. DAWN KEY/GETTY IMAGES

In the northwest corner of Colorado, the Sand Wash Basin horses make their home. They roam on about 158,000 acres (64,000 hectares) of land, most of it controlled by the BLM. When you tour this beautiful corner of the state, it's still possible to see the imprint of one of the most famous mustang stallions of all time, Picasso.

Picasso was born around 1990. In 2008, during a BLM roundup, someone saw the mature stallion and commented that his markings were like a painting by the artist Pablo Picasso. Somehow the name stuck, and before long thousands of people were coming to the Sand Wash Basin each year to get a glimpse of the beautiful stallion and his family. Various observers saw Picasso with different families over the years. He would put together a band of mares, then lose them to other stallions over time.

In 2018, when he would have been almost 30 years old, observers reported seeing him wandering alone, looking somewhat old and frail. Some of his admirers wanted to catch him and give him a comfortable place to live out the rest of his days, but most of his fans disagreed. He had lived his life like a king in the Sand Wash Basin. It was only right that he would end his life there too.

The last time anyone saw Picasso was November 2019. He's believed to have met his end somewhere under the splendid Sand Basin skies.

An Exmoor pony on the moor. Some people claim that the breed is descended directly from European wild horses.
ANGELA LOCK/SHUTTERSTOCK.COM

Four

Wild Horses Everywhere

MORE THAN THE MUSTANG

When most people in North America think about wild horses, what comes to mind is the American mustang. It has come to symbolize the wide open space of the American West as immortalized by countless movies, books and even a famous car.

But when it comes to wild horses, the American mustang is only a small slice of the whole picture. There are wild horses in almost every country of the world.

PRZEWALSKI'S HORSE

A Przewalski's horse (pronounced shuh-VAL-skee), scientifically known as *Equus ferus przewalskii* or sometimes *Equus przewalskii*, is one horse you will never see in a riding stable. They're rare and mean. They might look cute and fuzzy, but this isn't a horse you'd want as a pet. The Przewalski was long thought to be the last remaining actual wild horse. But recent DNA tests show that they do have some domestic blood as well.

They were named after the Russian geographer, explorer and army officer Nikolai Przewalski but are known in Mongolia as *takhi*, which means "spirit worthy of worship"— the ancient Mongolians considered them the mount of the gods. The horse is also known as Dzungarian horse, Asian wild horse and Mongolian wild horse. In the west, though, they are called Przewalski's horses, or P-horses for short.

By the mid-1960s there were only 134 Przewalski's horses held by 32 zoos and private collectors. Not long after this the last band of P-horses was spotted in the wild in Mongolia. No one knows for sure what happened— or even if they are still there. The ones in captivity have helped with the restoration of the species.

By 1990 there were over 1,000 P-horses at various zoos and institutions around the world. It was enough for a new start. Small bands of them have been released into the wild at different sites around the world. The populations are carefully monitored and the newly wild P-horses are doing well. The wild horses of the *steppes* are wild again!

KONIK HORSES

The last known tarpan or Eurasian wild horse, the last truly wild horse, died in a zoo in Russia early in the 20th century. The most successful of these attempts was the Polish-bred Konik.

The Konik physically resembles what we know of the tarpan, and for many years it was thought that the tarpan was, indeed, the ancestor of the Konik. But DNA testing showed that, despite a similar appearance, the Konik horse is not genetically related to the tarpan. Even so, the Konik has become the wild horse of choice for many *rewilding* and *conservation grazing* projects in Europe and the

Przewalski's horses in the Gobi Desert of Mongolia. PETR JAN JURAČKA—ZOO PRAHA/ WIKIMEDIA COMMONS/CC BY-SA 4.0

United Kingdom because the Konik is hardy and self-sufficient—it can be left on the range to fend for itself. There are around 1,150 free-ranging Konik horses at Oostvaardersplassen, a managed nature preserve in the Netherlands. At Wicken Fen in England there is a herd of about 100, and there are two herds—about 50 animals in total—that have been released in the Danube Delta. There are many other places where Konik horses are being used in rewilding programs.

Though you'll hear the Konik referred to as either a pony or horse, the Konik is a pony phenotype, as it is between 12 and 13.5 hands (4.3 feet or 130–140 centimeters), which is below what is considered standard horse size.

Konik horses have been used in several rewilding programs. This baby Konik is well protected by its fuzzy coat.
RICHARD EDELENBOS/DREAMSTIME.COM

A couple of young Konik stallions get into a scuffle. HANS VETH/UNSPLASH.COM

INDIA—THE WILD HORSES OF DIBRU-SAIKHOWA

There is a herd of about 80 horses in Dibru-Saikhowa National Park of Assam. Though they are a relatively small group, they are well loved. The park was designated as a *biosphere reserve* in 1997, making it an important cultural and recreational contribution to the Assam area. The horses are either descended from military horses who escaped during World War II or were left behind afterward. Unlike some of the other wild horses in the world, the future of the Dibru-Saikhowa National Park horses is secure.

The wild horses of the Dibru-Saikhowa biosphere reserve are well-loved and secure. SACHIN_BHARALI/SHUTTERSTOCK.COM

Brumbies in the Snowy Mountains, Kosciuszko National Park, Australia. CHRISTINE MENDOZA/UNSPLASH.COM

AUSTRALIA—THE BRUMBY

There is no history of horses in Australia before the early 1800s. That makes it all the more surprising that, of all the wild horse populations in the world, the Australian brumby is now the most numerous. Even the great wildfires of late 2019 and 2020 didn't threaten them. Today there are about 400,000 brumbies in Australia.

When the first European colonizers arrived in Australia in 1788, some of them brought horses with them. They were necessary in this huge and seemingly empty country. Horses were ridden to get around and they pulled carts and wagons. They were ridden for hunting and herding the cattle and sheep that the colonizers also brought with them.

Some people think the earliest feral horses in Australia escaped and began to run free. It is possible, though, that when machines became available to help with farming and other chores, some owners let the horses go rather than feed and care for them any longer.

New Zealand's Kaimanawa horses have a similar background to their brumby cousins in Australia. New Zealand, however, protects and manages its feral equine population. LYNTREE/SHUTTERSTOCK.COM

Two Garrano stallions fight in Portugal's Peneda-Gerês National Park (Parque Nacional da Peneda-Gerês).
NORBERTO ESTEVES/WIKIMEDIA COMMONS/CC BY-SA 4.0

Whatever the case, despite the harsh and unfamiliar conditions, the horses did well in Australia. They thrived. Australia's brumbies face some of the same challenges as America's wild horses because they compete with cattle and sheep on the open range.

PORTUGAL—THE GARRANO AND THE SORRAIA

Portugal's ancient Garrano—sometimes called the Minho—might be one of the oldest breeds of horses in existence. Cave drawings from the Paleolithic era—10,000 to 2.6 billion years ago—show a horse with the same short, stocky build and the same limited colors as they have today. Garranos are always chestnut or bay.

There are some Garranos in captivity. They make stable and sure-footed mounts and were at one time popular in racing. There are only 2,000 left in the wild, and their

numbers are declining, partly because of wolves in the areas where these horses roam.

The Sorraia is even older than the Garrano, and is almost certainly an ancestor, as are many European horse breeds. The breed no longer roams wild in Spain or Portugal, but experts think that at least some of the horses taken to North America by Columbus were Sorraia. One of the reasons for this is that the Sorraia's distinctive dun coat pattern and DNA showed up in the American mustang, in particular in the Kiger mustangs native to Oregon.

The position of both the Sorraia and the Garrano in the history of the modern horse is the subject of debate. We know for sure that both are ancient breeds, maybe more closely related to the P-horse and extinct wild *Equus* species than to modern breeds.

Sorraia horses in the Middle Coa Valley in northern Portugal. JUAN CARLOS MUNOZ/ SHUTTERSTOCK.COM

The Banker horses, or Banker ponies, as they are variously known, make their home on the Outer Banks of North Carolina. KEVINCOLLINS123/WIKIMEDIA COMMONS/CC BY-SA 3.0

BANKER HORSES

No, these are not horses who are super good at math! Rather, Bankers are the wild horses who make their home on the barrier islands off the coast of North Carolina. The area is known as the Outer Banks, which is how the horses got their name.

And, in the memory of North Carolinians, the horses have "always" been there. They can be found on Currituck Banks (Corolla), Ocracoke Island, Shackleford Banks and in the Rachel Carson Reserve. The US National Park Service keeps its eyes on the 400-plus wild horses that roam these popular resort areas. The horses are thought to be descendants of horses that were shipwrecked or abandoned during early Spanish explorations of the area in the 1500s.

THE AMERICAN BURRO

A few years ago my husband and I headed out by car to find a hot-springs resort in rural Arizona. We got off the highway to head into Lake Pleasant Regional Park. After a while we passed the lake, crossed over a **cattle guard** and found ourselves in some pretty wild country.

We rounded a corner, and I screeched in surprise and delight: "Stop the car!" I scooted out, phone in pocket, camera around my neck, and headed straight for what turned out to be the Lake Pleasant wild burros. "Be careful," my husband warned as I scampered away. And, of course, one always must be careful with wild animals. But oh! How charming were these two! A young *jenny* and her foal, watching me curiously, long ears alert.

Wild burros can be found in California, Nevada, Arizona, Utah and Oregon. And although burro and donkey are the same animal, some people say a burro is simply a donkey who lives in the West.
TWILDLIFE/GETTY IMAGES

A Little Help from Some Swimmy Friends

Sable Island horses crop the sparse seaside grass that makes up most of their diet.
JULIE MARSHALL/SHUTTERSTOCK.COM

For generations the population of the Sable Island horses had remained around a steady 200 to 400. A few years ago a biologist at the University of Saskatchewan noted that the population had risen to 450 to 550 horses—the new normal. What was going on?

Philip McLoughlin and his team showed a connection between the growing number of Sable Island horses and the burgeoning seal populations on Canada's East Coast. The number of gray seals in the waters around Sable Island has grown from less than 1,000 in the 1960s to almost 400,000 today. Gray seals give birth on the island, fertilizing the once-barren grasslands and causing the sparse grasses to grow into a never-ending food supply for the horses.

"What is really interesting," says McLoughlin, "is that we show how the enrichment of grasses…affects how the horses move around the island to eat."

Every year, however, 50 to 60 Sable Island horses die from starvation and hypothermia. The population may be growing overall, but it's a difficult life for those that survive, out there on this island 180 miles (290 kilometers) southeast of Halifax.

The Sable Island horses have been protected by the Canada Shipping Act since 1961. In the 1950s, seen as a threat to the ecology, they were captured and shipped away to work in  mines or be killed for their meat and hides. Thousands of Canadian schoolchildren wrote to the prime minister of the time, John Diefenbaker, pleading that the horses not be captured for work, meat or glue. Today no one may remove horses from the island.

I would take a photo and inch closer. Take another photo and inch closer still.

The jenny tolerated this for a bit, but when I got too close, she turned tail and ran, her foal obediently at her side. It wasn't long before we saw the rest of their herd. I was beside myself with joy.

I had always thought burros to be tiny and sturdy. These looked tall and elegant to me, although my later research let me know they are only about 12 hands (48 inches or 122 centimeters) and 350 pounds (159 kilograms). The burros of the western United States all have a similar backstory. They were brought from Spain as early as the 16th century to help the priests who had come to try to convert the Indigenous Peoples to Christianity. The priests intended to cover a lot of ground, and they didn't need to go super fast, so burros were more ideal and less fussy than horses. (Like choosing a sturdy gas-saving compact car over a sports car. They just wanted to get there. Eventually.)

There is something entirely charming in the expressive face of a donkey.
LUCAFABBIAN/DREAMSTIME.COM

Wild burros and donkeys are all *Equus africanus asinus*, as they are all descended from African asses. The BLM estimates there are currently about 16,000 wild burros in the United States. But just what is a burro? A burro is a donkey. Full stop. In fact, *burro* is the Spanish word for donkey. Donkeys are noble beasts! They were probably first bred around 5,000 years ago in Egypt or Mesopotamia.

A burro should not be confused with a mule. Mules are always **hybrid**. A mule is the offspring of a female horse and a male donkey (a jack—hence the word *jackass*). The offspring of donkeys and horses are always sterile. They can't ever have offspring of their own.

THE SACRED HORSES OF THE AMERICAS

Yvette Running Horse Collin, who we first met in chapter 3, is from the Oglala Lakota Nation. She has traveled to several states and into Canada, gathering the 100-plus horses in her care at Sacred Way Sanctuary, the nonprofit organization she co-founded and helps run in rural Alabama.

Collin says that the horses at Sacred Way, as well as those she's placed in homes outside of the sanctuary, display unique traits and characteristics that indicate ancient blood reflective of the Indigenous cultures they are associated with. Collin says that about half of the horses in her care originated from the Native American tribal lines of the southern United States, including Choctaw, Cherokee and Chickasaw. The horses she has collected also include Native American horse lines such as the Lakota, Nakota, Cheyenne, Mayan, Kiowa, Apache, Ojibwe, Mohawk, Ute and Pueblo.

"As our traditions record and archeology has validated, all horses originated in the Americas. The horses husbanded and protected by Indigenous Peoples exhibited unique characteristics, and they are distinctly different than heavily domesticated breeds," Collin says, referencing the distinguishing markings on some horses and exceptionally curly hair on others. These are traits she says have followed these horses from a time before history.

Collin says that at a core level Indigenous Peoples interacted with horses in a different way than Europeans have. "Horses were never beasts of burden," Collin says.

The annual pony swim helps cull the two herds of ponies on Assateague Island to keep their population in check.
UNITED STATES COAST GUARD, PA2 CHRISTOPHER EVANSON/WIKIMEDIA COMMONS/PUBLIC DOMAIN

"We understood them to be sacred relatives." Collin calls them "medicine horses." In line with her traditions, she never sells horses. Rather, some of these special horses have been gifted to people to help cure ills and strengthen bonds. "The horses always help us, and in return we protect and stand for them," says Collin.

For most of the year, the ponies on Assateague Island live a wild life, often foraging or, as seen here, relaxing.
ASCHEN/GETTY IMAGES

CHINCOTEAGUE PONY

The Chincoteague pony was immortalized by the award-winning book *Misty of Chincoteague*, by Marguerite Henry. It was published in 1947 and has never been out of print since.

The famous Chincoteague ponies are found on Assateague Island. One herd is in Maryland and the other in Virginia. There have been wild ponies on Assateague Island for hundreds of years. Though no one is sure quite where they came from, local people believe that all the ponies in the region are descended from the equine survivors of a Spanish galleon that wrecked off the coast of Assateague. Some people think the ancestors of the current ponies were released by colonists trying to get out of paying taxes on their livestock. Maybe both things are true. Wherever they came from, today these ponies are greatly loved by their local humans. An annual pony swim and adoption creatively manages the size of the herd by bringing horses into the community while keeping the wild herd at a manageable size.

WILD HORSES OF THE UNITED KINGDOM

The earliest evidence of the equine species in the United Kingdom dates back to 700,000 BCE, during the Pleistocene epoch. There is evidence that by 500,000 BCE humans were hunting the ancestors of the wild horse. During that time, the area that is now called the United Kingdom was connected to Europe by a land bridge similar to the one that connected Alaska and Russia in prehistory. So from that time until about 9,000 years ago, horses, humans and all other animals could travel between Europe and the UK.

Most of the wild horses in the UK today are ancient breeds that have been reintroduced in areas where wild horses once roamed. In Wales and other places, wild horses are being used to bring the land they roam back to

A herd of wild Welsh ponies in North Wales. RAJ KAMAL/GETTY IMAGES

its natural state (see "Conservation Grazing" sidebar in chapter 5).

Some people claim that the Carneddau ponies in northwestern Wales are the only truly wild horses left in the United Kingdom. Research has shown that they are genetically distinct. Around 300 ponies roam the Carneddau Mountains in Snowdonia National Park. Their ancestors have been there since the Bronze Age.

More than 700 Shetland ponies roam wild in Snowdonia National Park in Wales. IVANMATTIOLI/DREAMSTIME.COM

The beautiful and famous Fell and Dales ponies of the Pennines are wild as well, though conservationists have helped preserve them by breeding them with other types of horses over the years. This helped create *genetic diversity* and increased the dwindling numbers of these two threatened breeds.

Though the tiny and adorable-looking Shetland ponies that roam the island of Foula appear to run wild, each pony is actually owned by the *crofters* who live there. Thirty-eight people live on Foula, the most remote of the inhabited islands in the United Kingdom. The island is about 4.9 square miles (12.6 kilometers) and is home to over 1,500 Shetland ponies.

THE CAMARGUE

For as long as anyone can remember, small, hardy wild horses have lived in the Camargue marshes and wetlands of the Rhône delta in France. It's been the home of these horses for possibly thousands of years.

The origins of this ancient breed are unknown, though they are thought to be closely related to the Spanish Barb and other horses from Iberia. Julius Caesar and Napoleon are both said to have admired the Camargue's sturdy nature and strength and selected some of the horses for their armies.

Like gray horses everywhere, Camargue horses are born black or brown and their coats lighten as they age. By full adulthood they will always be a beautiful silver color.

By the time he is fully adult, this young Camargue horse will be the distinctive silver-white the breed is known for.
SERGEY URYADNIKOV/DREAMSTIME.COM

Camargue horses gallop through water in the swamps of the Regional Nature Park of the Camargue (Parc naturel régional de Camargue) in Provence, France.
SERGEY URYADNIKOV/DREAMSTIME.COM

Thousands of horses run free in Iceland in the summer months. There are 350,000 people in Iceland, plus 80,000 horses. But only about 100 of those horses are wild.
VERVERIDIS VASILIS/SHUTTERSTOCK.COM

ASSES

Asses include several horse-related species, including onagers, kulans and donkeys, known for either their wildness or—in the domestic varieties—their endurance. Asses have long ears, a coarse mane and tail, and stocky, straight bodies. And asses lack the **withers** seen in horses. Asses are mentioned here because there are several wild species, and they *are* members of the genus *Equus*. But the mention is brief because they are not the wild horses we're thinking about.

The onager is also known as hemione or Asiatic wild ass. It is native to Asia.
T.VOEKLER/WIKIMEDIA COMMONS/CC BY-SA 3.0

ZEBRAS

Are zebras really horses? Well…yes and no. It's complicated! One thing they are not is horses with stripes. They are very different, inside and out. While Przewalski's horse has some **chromosomal** differences from domestic horses, if they are interbred, they can produce offspring that are not sterile. The same is not true for zebras—zebra and horse crosses are always sterile.

All three extant species of zebras are of the genus *Equus*. Zebra manes are short and coarse, and their tails are bare on top with a tuft at the end, like that of an ass or a lion.

And zebras have never been domesticated, even though a few have been slightly tamed over the years. Zebras are truly wild. Filmmakers came face-to-face with that reality while making the 2005 movie *Racing Stripes*, featuring Frankie Muniz, David Spade, Snoop Dogg…and a zebra. In the film, a circus zebra named Stripes dreams of becoming a racehorse, and (spoiler alert!) ultimately his dream comes true. Of course, none of this was anywhere

A Grant's zebra mother and foal. Grant's zebras are the smallest of the plains zebras.
TALKS PRESENTERS 09/WIKIMEDIA COMMONS/CC BY-SA 3.0

near possible. Seven zebras were made available to play Stripes. The two tamest were chosen—except for the racing scenes. The animal who played Stripes in the racing scenes was a horse with zebra stripes painted on. What gives it away? If you look closely at those scenes, you'll see a horsetail on the racing animal who is supposed to be Stripes.

Today there are fewer than 1,000 Somali wild asses (*Equus asinus somalicus*) in the world.
REYNOLD MAINSE/DESIGN PICS/GETTY IMAGES

Why Do Zebras Have Stripes?

NAOMI CATTAN/GETTY IMAGES

Do zebras have stripes to fool predators? To help them keep cool? To let each other know who they are? None of the above. But it turns out there's an answer that researchers had long suspected but have now proven to be true—zebra stripes are there to confuse biting insects like horseflies and tsetse flies.

A 2020 study at the University of Bristol in England proved that horseflies would fly right over zebras and land on horses instead. Or they'd try to land on the zebras but end up bumping into them or zooming around pointlessly, unable to land.

To prove that it really was the stripes causing the confusion, not just something about the zebras themselves, researchers dressed the horses like zebras. No, really! They put zebra-striped blankets on the horses. The result? You guessed it—the horseflies would collide with the dressed-up horses or fly over them.

From living on the open plains to confinement in BLM corrals and sanctuaries and even to adoption, today's mustangs have more challenges than ever before.
LORI SORTINO/ESSENCE CAPTURED PHOTOGRAPHY

Five

The Modern Mustang

WILD HORSES AND THE ENVIRONMENT

As we've discovered, wild horse supporters and some scientists say that the way herds graze and migrate benefits the ranges where they live. Those who would like to see the wild herds exterminated or greatly reduced maintain that wild horses ruin the rangeland.

Since both sides have convincing arguments, it's difficult for decision makers to know who is right, especially since the things said by one side often contradict what the other side claims. What do you think? Here are a few claims made by both people who support wild horses and those who don't.

The Good

- Wild horses provide a diet for predators.
- Horse manure enriches and fertilizes the soil.
- Wild horses enhance the areas where they graze by making local resources more accessible for other species.
- The presence of wild horses enhances native plant life by spreading seeds.
- Wild horses reduce the possibility of fire by clearing debris that might feed a fire.
- Wild horses can have a positive impact on the communities nearest their ranges through tourism.

The Bad

- Wild horses have no natural predators.
- When it isn't managed properly, horse manure can pollute the environment.
- Wild horse populations threaten other wild species by overusing local resources or using up all the food and water.
- Wild horses overgraze native plants.
- Wild horses produce methane, which contributes to climate change and wildfires.
- Wild horses detract from the financial communities nearest them due to their impact on livestock grazing.

Between 700,000 and 1.9 million head of livestock—sheep and cattle—currently graze on land managed by the Bureau of Land Management (BLM) in the United States, at a cost to the ranchers of $1.35 per head per month. That's quite a bit less than it costs to feed a dog or cat and about a tenth of the cost of grazing the same livestock on private land. Contrast that with the maximum (currently) of 80,000 mustangs grazing the same land. The BLM aims to reduce that number to the mid-1970s level of 26,000 horses—a number that even then was considered well below ideal and far below historic numbers.

The fact that far more cattle than horses are allowed to graze has not escaped the attention of wild horse advocates. Hearings, petitions and lawsuits are ongoing. As much as getting wild horses off the range might benefit some ranchers, North America's wild horses are beloved by many, and the fight continues.

EQUINE FIREFIGHTERS

Wild horses can help curb the negative effects of climate change. Is it a coincidence that the states where wildfire damage has been the most severe in recent years are also the ones where the most wild horses have been removed from the range? Some experts don't think so.

There is some evidence that a wild horse will eat five and a half tons (five metric tons) of "fire fodder" every year. Some people say that releasing all the wild horses currently being held by the BLM back into the wild would significantly reduce the effects of wildfires.

In 2014, rancher and naturalist William E. Simpson II began a seven-year study of how horses help prevent

A beautiful bay mare at Return to Freedom sanctuary.
LORI SORTINO/ESSENCE CAPTURED PHOTOGRAPHY

forest fires. Simpson got the idea when he read other studies reporting that if there are enough grazing animals put in an area prone to forest fires, fewer and less intense wildfires will occur. Simpson put together a wild horse fire brigade to help combat the horrendous wildfires in California. The hope is that they can combat fires before they even begin.

Simpson's project introduces wild horses to forests and fields. The idea is that the horses will eat some of the smaller branches, leaves and other things that can lead to bigger fires. It costs much less to bring wild horses to remote areas than it does to bring firefighting equipment there. And the bonus is, it gives wild horses a new and valuable job.

Horses don't need to be taught any special skills in order to be good at fire prevention. Their natural habit of grazing and browsing helps clear the forest of burnable material.
LORI SORTINO/ESSENCE CAPTURED PHOTOGRAPHY

Helicopter roundups can be frightening and dangerous.
BLM NEVADA/FLICKR.COM/CC BY-SA 2.0

WILD HORSE MANAGEMENT

The BLM manages wild horses and burros in 177 herd-management areas (HMAs) across 10 western states. These areas have different local climates, natural resources and geography. At the same time, each herd has its own history, genetic heritage, size distribution and, in some cases, coloring. It is challenging to manage so many different animals and situations. Critics of the BLM aren't always sure the organization is doing a good job of meeting that challenge, and even wonder sometimes if the best interests of the animals are really being served.

The registered nonprofit Cloud Foundation, based in Colorado and founded by award-winning filmmaker Ginger Kathrens, has been one of the most vocal critics of the BLM, actively and frequently calling out the organization and accusing it of such things as "managing America's wild horses into extinction." The Cloud Foundation isn't the only group that feels that way. Laura Leigh, founder of Wild Horse Education, recently said that what the BLM is doing "is not management; it is insanity. The damage will last for decades."

How to Adopt a Wild Horse or Burro

SARAH BECKWITH, BUREAU OF LAND MANAGEMENT

Do you feel like your life will not be complete unless you have your very own mustang? Well, first off, give it lots of thought! Even if you have a big property (and horses *do* need room to roam), horses are a lot of work, none more so than one who was born in the wild. The horse will need training, and so will you, so make sure you're really ready to take on this new four-hoofed mouth to feed.

But if you *are* ready and you've checked with your parents and they've said, "Go!," there are a couple of good places to start your research. Every year the Bureau of Land Management (BLM) sponsors special sales and adoption programs to find homes for the horses they've removed from the range to help control herd populations.

Would-be purchasers can find detailed information online, but must fill out an adoption application in order to bid. Successful bidders can pay anywhere from $125 to a few thousand dollars for the most desirable individuals—horses that have special colors or markings or have received some training through the BLM.

In the past sales were held at designated locations. More recently online sales have been added, with potential buyers able to see detailed information about the various horses, including where they were captured and what level of training they have had.

He halted, half turned, and snorted

A.S.Havell.

Vintage engraving of cowboys herding wild horses on the American plains in the 1880s.
DUNCAN1890/GETTY IMAGES

HOME ON THE RANGE

Wild horses in the United States are roaming on just under 27 million acres (11 million hectares). As a few points of comparison, New York's famous Central Park covers 843 acres (341 hectares), and Vancouver's huge and lovely Stanley Park is 1,000 acres (405 hectares). Western Canada's giant jewel of a park, Banff National Park, is 1.64 million acres (664,100 hectares), and Yellowstone National Park is 2.222 million acres (900,000 hectares). And if you've been to any of those places, you know you could stash a whole lot of wild horses in any of them. So nearly 27 million acres? That's a lot.

Wild horses at Monument Valley, near the Arizona-Utah border.
KARL HENDON/GETTY IMAGES

The BLM claims that in 1971, when the Wild Free-Roaming Horses and Burros Act was created, mustang numbers had been reduced to 25,345 horses in total. At the time, wild horse supporters thought this number meant the animals' existence was threatened.

The BLM has an ideal number in mind for wild horses and burros in the West. They recently said that the "appropriate management level" number is 26,690 wild horses and burros on western public rangelands. As you can see, there is a difference between the ideal number and the actual number, and an even greater difference between those numbers and what wild horse protectors would like to see.

Horses and birds enjoy a symbiotic relationship. Birds eat the flies that horses attract, and the horses enjoy an existence that is more bug-free. The birds also get a free ride!
JOSEPH KEIL/UNSPLASH.COM

ENTER THE PROTECTORS

Many people and organizations are fighting for the future of the American mustang. Some of those organizations have been mentioned already in this book. There are the American Wild Horse Campaign, Return to Freedom, Cloud Foundation, Blue Equus and many other advocacy and rescue groups. While they are all opposed to what the BLM is doing, they don't all agree with each other—in either numbers or methods—on how to protect wild horses.

One of the biggest debates is on how to control the population. There are three main options:

Many organizations and individuals are dedicated to protecting America's wild horses. But they don't always agree on the best method of doing that.
LORI SORTINO/ESSENCE CAPTURED PHOTOGRAPHY

1. **Round up and sell** the number of horses that exceeds the ideal number decided upon by the BLM. If individual horses are too old or mean to be sold, keep them in a big field to live their lives out comfortably but not really in the wild.

2. **Let nature take its course.** That means that, every year, some horses would be eaten by predators, some would die of starvation or dehydration because there wouldn't be enough resources around, etc.

3. **Administer some form of contraceptive** to control the number of foals born every year.

The roundups are the method currently being used, along with a relatively small amount of horse birth control. The roundups are also the approach that seems to

A herd of wild mustangs being rounded up at dawn. WORLDWIDEIMAGES/GETTY IMAGES

make almost no one happy. It apparently costs taxpayers US$50 million to run the program each year. Horses are often rounded up by helicopter, and animals are often injured, sometimes even euthanized. It's barbaric and, critics say, unnecessary.

No group of any size seems to be advocating to let nature take its course, because, as sensible as that approach might sound in theory, no one wants to see starving, dying horses on the range.

The contraceptive route has been tested on and approved for wild horses. A vaccine that has proven to be safe and effective has been in use for over 30 years. Mares are darted from a distance, and the vaccine works for up to five years. In 2021, a total of 1,160 horses received the contraceptive. But 13,666 wild horses were rounded up and removed from the range.

The BLM argues that darting is not a viable option for most wild horse herds because the animals tend to avoid human contact, and the vast sizes of most herd management areas make it difficult to locate and approach individual horses. However, since the horses are being rounded up in huge numbers anyway, some people say it makes sense to conduct population-control roundups, where mares are darted and then released.

Wild horses face off at McCullough Peaks Wild Horse Herd Management Area in Wyoming. RINUS BAAK/DREAMSTIME.COM

Conservation Grazing

LINDA L. RICHARDS

Critics of free-ranging horses in North America say that wild horses have a negative impact on the environment. In other parts of the world, the impact of wild horses on the environment is not only welcomed, it's engineered.

For example, in England and other parts of the United Kingdom, horses are used for conservation grazing, a practice that relies on their appetites to help the environment.

Conservationists have gone so far as to import wild horses from other countries in order to restore local environments to the way they were before humans arrived and messed things up with farming and development. In areas where there is annual threat of fire, conservation grazing effectively clears burnable debris from grazing areas.

The Broads is a national park in England that covers over 117 square miles (303 square kilometers) and is home to a quarter of the most rare species of animals in the United Kingdom, including water voles, cuckoos and European eels.

The Broads also has a team of 25 conservation grazers, a mix of Konik and Welsh ponies, including a few rescue ponies. Park authorities call their ponies the "munch bunch." Because horses are selective grazers, they choose to eat certain plants and generally prefer grasses and other fine-leaved species. The ponies range freely and choose where they want to eat. Some vegetation is eaten short, some just nibbled, and other areas are not eaten at all. This selective munching results in different habitats, creating ideal conditions for diverse plants and animals.

The horses that make their home along the
Salt River in Tonto National Forest near Phoenix are
protected by state law. Viewing them is a popular
tourist activity. VLAD GEORGESCU/GETTY IMAGES

LOOKING INTO THE FUTURE

With so much discussion about removing horses from public lands, one of the things that often gets overlooked is that there other answers. Maybe some of the old ways need to make way for the new.

For instance, a 2020 poll revealed that 23 percent of adults in the United States claim to have reduced the amount of meat they consume. With that in mind, a system that supports the beef industry and enriches a handful of ranchers does not reflect the needs of a modern society. Maybe wild horses don't have to compete against ranchers for land as much as they once did.

Additionally, wild horses have the potential to generate income that will benefit entire regions through ecotourism. People love to see wild horses in their natural habitat. Also, compared to viewing big wild bears or cats, seeing horses in the wild is relatively safe—as long as you keep your distance.

And there are already some big success stories. The Pryor Mountain Wild Mustang Center, just east of Lovell, Wyoming, has been repeatedly voted best attraction in the state by *USA Today*. The Salt River Wild Horse Management Group is an Arizona-based nonprofit dedicated to monitoring, studying and protecting the Salt River wild horses of Tonto National Forest, about an hour outside of Phoenix. The organization believes the horses bring tens of thousands of visitors to Tonto National Forest every year who would not otherwise have come.

One of the real positives the future might bring, then, is the realization across wild horse advocacy groups that

The potential of wild horses to bring income into an area through tourism has not yet been fully explored. But people love horses—especially when they're running free. And they enjoy the opportunity to see them up close.
EBERHARD GROSSGASTEIGER/UNSPLASH.COM

Digging Wells in the Desert

In 2014 Erick Lundgren, a field ecologist working in Arizona's Sonoran Desert, observed wild donkeys digging wells to access drinking water. It made him wonder if other animals in the area were also using the wells. Lundgren and his team of researchers monitored the wells for several summers and discovered that 59 different species came to drink from or investigate the new wells that had been dug. The wells didn't just provide water, though. The researchers found that nearby trees and vegetation benefitted from the wells' wet soil.

This is the first study done of the well-digging behavior, but it's not the first report. Wild donkeys and horses have been observed digging wells in Australia, on Sable Island and in the Gobi Desert. These engineering animals are not entirely unique either. Coyotes and elephants also dig wells, and beavers can change their environment to make things better for themselves.

building a case together for the economic benefit wild horses can bring to their communities on a regional and state level might go a long way in protecting the herds.

COMING HOME

Part of what people love about wild horses is what they represent. Even in cases where their ancestors weren't born in that part of the world, they have imprinted themselves on the spirit of the people and on the land.

Winston Churchill, prime minister of England during World War II, said that there "is something about the outside of a horse that is good for the inside of a man." Horses reflect our humanity. They show us the best parts of ourselves and make us want to be better. (And by "man," in this instance, I've always thought he meant all people.)

Horses are special, is what I think he meant.

There may always be debates about wild horses and whether they help or hinder the environment, whether the rangeland they graze would be better off given to cattle so ranchers can make more money. But the horses themselves endure, in one way or another, with no concern at all about what we think.

The Australian poet Pam Brown said, "A horse is the projection of people's dreams about themselves—strong, powerful, beautiful—and it has the capability of giving us escape from our mundane existence."

Wild horses are all of that and more. They whisper to us about the possibility of real freedom. Preserving them in the wild gives us hope.

A peaceful scene at sunset.
LORI SORTINO/ESSENCE CAPTURED PHOTOGRAPHY

Glossary

alpha—in animals, the dominant member of a group and generally the boss of the others

ancestor species—a species from which modern equivalents have descended

ass—a small member of the horse family with long ears and a distinctive call; also known as donkey or burro

band—another word for herd, which is a horse family usually consisting of a stallion, mares and foals

beta—in animals, the second-in-command of the herd or group

biosphere reserve—official designation given to an ecosystem with plants and animals of unusual scientific and natural interest

blaze—a strip of white on the face of a horse

browser—an animal that feeds on leaves, shoots and the fruit of shrubs

Bureau of Land Management (BLM)—the agency within the US Department of the Interior that manages outdoor recreation, livestock grazing, mineral development and energy production on public lands

cattle guard—an obstacle to prevent livestock from moving through an open gateway on a piece of fenced land. Bars are placed over a shallow open pit. The gaps are wide enough for an animal's feet to fall through but narrow enough to allow vehicles and people on foot to cross safely; also known as cattle grid and stock grid

chromosomal—of chromosomes, which are the tiny, threadlike structures located in the cells of plants and animals. Each chromosome is made of protein and a DNA molecule.

colt—a young male horse

conservation grazing—the use of livestock (wild, feral or domestic) to improve and maintain wildlife and plant habitat

crofters—a term from the United Kingdom referring to people who rent and work small plots of land called *crofts*

DNA—abbreviation for deoxyribonucleic acid, the hereditary material in cells that determines the features of each species

dominant—commanding or controlling all others because of superior strength or power

dorsal stripe—a black stripe that a dun horse has down its back

epoch—a period of time in history marked by distinctive features or key developments

equids—members of the family Equidae, which includes horses, asses and zebras

equine—relating to or affecting equids

extant—still in existence

extinction event—a widespread and rapid decrease in the biodiversity on the earth, causing whole species to disappear; also known as mass extinction or biotic crisis

feral—a plant or animal that lives in the wild but is descended from domesticated individuals

fillies—young female horses

foal—a horse or donkey up to one year old

forbs—broad-leafed herbs other than grass

genetic diversity—the range of different inherited traits within a species

genus—a group of related species

hand—a unit of measure equal to 4 inches (10 centimeters), used for the height of horses

harem—a group of female animals with the same male mate

herbaceous—having the characteristics of herbs; nonwoody

herd—a group of animals that live, feed and migrate together

hybrids—animals that are the offspring of two plants or animals of different species

invasive—spreading quickly or aggressively. Invasive species of plants and animals grow easily in non-native environments, often usurping local species.

jenny—adult female donkey

mare—adult female horse

neutered—altered so that the animal cannot reproduce

phenotype—the observable characteristics of an organism (how it looks and behaves) that result from the interaction of its genes and its environment

points—the mane, tail, lower legs and ear rims, which are black on a bay horse

predators—animals that naturally prey on others

retina—the light-sensitive layer of tissue at the back of the eyeball

rewilding—returning habitats to a natural state, repairing damaged ecosystems and restoring degraded landscapes

sedges—plants in the Cyperaceae family. Like grasses, sedges tend to form in either dense clumps or tufts, but they usually have three-sided stems and leaves. They also have thick, fibrous roots or tuber-like underground stems.

slaughtered—killed

stallion—adult male horse that is not neutered

stay apparatus—the group of muscles, tendons and ligaments that lock the major limbs so an animal can remain standing with virtually no muscular effort

steppes—large areas of flat, unforested grassland

symbiotic—characterized by a relationship or connection between two organisms that aren't the same species

ungulate—a hoofed mammal. Cattle, pigs, giraffes, camels, deer and—yes—horses are all examples of ungulates.

withers—the highest part of a horse's back, located between the shoulder blades. A horse's height is measured from the ground at the front foot to the withers.

Resources

PRINT

Boyd, Lee, and Katherine A. Houpt. *Przewalski's Horse: The History and Biology of an Endangered Species*. SUNY Press, 1994.

Chow, Lily. *Chasing Their Dreams*. Caitlin Press, 2001.

Cruise, David, and Alison Griffiths. *Wild Horse Annie and the Last of the Mustangs: The Life of Velma Johnston*. Scribner, 2013.

Fitch, R.T. *Straight from the Horse's Heart: A Spiritual Ride through Love, Loss and Hope*. BookSurge, 2009.

Harris, Moira C. *Wild Horses of the World*. Hamlyn, 2009.

Philipps, David. *Wild Horse Country: The History, Myth, and Future of the Mustang*. W.W. Norton, 2017.

Pomeranz, Lynne. *Among Wild Horses: A Portrait of the Pryor Mountain Mustangs*. Storey Publishing, 2006.

ONLINE

Adopt A Wild Horse: blm.gov/programs/wild-horse-and-burro/adoptions-and-sales

American Wild Horse Campaign: americanwildhorsecampaign.org

American Wild Horse Campaign Map: americanwildhorsecampaign.org/media/where-view-wild-horses-and-burros-map

Benjamin Burger YouTube channel: youtube.com/c/BenjaminBurgerScience?app=desktop

Bureau of Land Management: blm.gov

Cloud Foundation: thecloudfoundation.org

Corolla Wild Horse Fund: obxguides.com/corolla-outer-banks/corollawildhorsemuseum

Hanaeleh: hanaeleh.org/wild-mustangs

"The Horse Gene Map" in Ilar Journal: academic.oup.com/ilarjournal/article/39/2-3/171/624009

Nokota Horse Conservancy: nokotahorse.org

Pryor Mountain Wild Mustang Center: pryormustangs.org

The Quagga Project: quaggaproject.org

Return to Freedom: returntofreedom.org

The Wild Free-Roaming Horses and Burros Act of 1971: blm.gov/sites/blm.gov/files/programs_wildhorse_history_doc1.pdf

Acknowledgments

I tried really hard to get everything in this book right and include all the things I wanted to tell you about, but it was so difficult! I'm pretty sure I've left out some important stuff, and it will come to me weeks after it's too late to change anything. If that happens, and you notice, forgive me, please. Also know that if something is wrong, it is entirely my fault and not that of the tremendous people who have assisted with every step of my work.

You won't have to read very far to understand that talking about wild horses in North America is controversial. A lot of people disagree even about the simplest issues. Are mustangs wild or feral? Do they belong on the range or in a pen? Do they have a right to live at all? I hope I have given you some of the tools you need to decide these things for yourself.

Thank you to everyone who helped put this book into your hands. My patient and talented editor, Kirstie Hudson, played a really big part in all that is good about this book. From the first she was enthusiastic about the project and stuck by me and was supportive even when the going was tough. (And the going got quite tough!) The whole team at Orca is so astonishing and were also unbelievably patient and gentle with me. They are such a talented bunch. Thank you.

Professional equine photographer Lori Sortino was very supportive. Her suggestions were wonderful, and as you can see, her photos are amazing.

Dr. Benjamin Burger, associate professor of geology at Utah State University, was very generous with his time in looking over the section on the origins of the horse. If anything is wrong, it's my fault, but his passion and clarity on the subject helped me get a lot of it straight. (Also, please look for his YouTube channel. When it comes to the real history of the animals that walked the earth, no one tells it better.)

Thanks as always to my husband, Anthony J. Parkinson; my son, Michael Karl Richards; and my brother, Dr. Peter Huber. In very different ways the three of you are essential ingredients to everything that is beautiful in my life. (And there's a lot!)

In the course of writing this book, I talked to many people. I'm not going to thank them in this space individually, but their voices are here: they are passionate and reflective of the horses they feel so strongly about.

Index

*Page numbers in **bold** indicate an image caption.*

JEANNIE LEE

LINDA L. RICHARDS is the award-winning author of 16 books, including *Return from Extinction: The Triumph of the Elephant Seal*. Linda is from Vancouver, British Columbia, and currently makes her home in Phoenix. She's an accomplished horsewoman and avid tennis player, and she enjoys yoga, hiking, cooking and playing guitar, though not at the same time. Linda loves asking questions that are obvious in order to get answers that are unexpected. Sometimes when she does that a lot, she ends up writing a book, because the answers are so surprising that she wants to share them.